COMPILED BY SHARICE PORTER

Copyright © 2021 by Sharice Porter

All rights reserved. No part of this publication may be reproduced in any form or by any means, electronic or mechanical, including photocopying or recording, without the prior written consent of the publisher.

Published and Printed in the United States
Print versions may vary.
Edited by Edna_pro_editor - via Fiverr

Cover and Book Design by Elev8ted Graphic Design
www.Elev8tedGraphics.com
Facebook and Instagram @elev8tedgraphics
Twitter - @DesignElev8ted

ISBN 978-1-7368958-0-1

ACKNOWLEDGEMENT

We would like to acknowledge Nakia Austin, M.A. for her vision in creating the 100 Healed Movement and her amazing leadership over the 100 Healed Ambassadors.

THANK YOU

Contents

Chapter 1 — *Angels in Disguise-Misunderstandings in Communication* - By Sharice Porter
Page 9

Chapter 2 — *My Heart is Safe with My Sisters - Maintaining Friendships Through Empathy and Emotional Honesty* - By Bridgette Smith
Page 19

Chapter 3 — *Embracing Who You Are- Misunderstandings and Jealousy* - By Charity Todd
Page 27

Chapter 4 — *Be Authentically You!* - By Stephanie Cherise Bell
Page 37

Chapter 5 — *Closed Minds Don't Get Fed* - By Polita Boyde
Page 45

Chapter 6 — *Girl Put Yourself Out There- Stop Denying the World of How Fabulous You Are* - By Sonjia Lindsey
Page 55

Chapter 7 — *The Divine Gift of Godly Relationships* - By Tempy Douglas
Page 63

Chapter 1

Angels in Disguise
Misunderstandings in Communication

By Sharice Porter

"Friends, how many of us have them? Friends, ones we can depend on..." How many of you remember the lyrics to that Whodini song from the 1980s? Thankfully, I can say that the answer to both questions is yes. I have them and I can depend on them. I have had the same friends since junior high school. I have heard women say it is difficult to have friendships with other women. That statement is strange to me. I have never had that issue. I have even heard my younger sister say the same thing. When I hear that, I think the problem is not with the other women. The problem is with the person making the statement. My friendships have all started easy and have remained organic and true over the years. I cannot say that my friends and I have never had disagreements, but we have been able to resolve every issue that has come up. Each of my friends have different personalities, but we all mix very well.

My oldest and dearest friend came around shortly after I started the sixth grade. My mom had suffered from a brain aneurysm when I was in the fifth grade. I kept that information from my new friend because I decided it was easier to wear the mask that everything was ok than to open the flood gates to my life. I did not know that she was wearing a mask of her own. Her grandmother was raising her. I never asked why. As our relationship evolved, she opened up to me, making it easy for me to open up to her. It was as if our hearts needed one another. We were able to share our problems with each other. It was the first time in my life that I felt like I had someone willing to hold my secrets. In turn, I held hers. I would stay at her house often. I needed her sunshine when my skies at home were gray. I was happy to have somewhere to go just to get away from my life, even if it was just for a moment. We were vulnerable with each other. I opened my door to her, and she opened hers to me. It was the first time that I could let some of the baggage that I carried daily go.

Over the years, she was there for all the pivotal moments of my life. She taught me how to drive in her beat-up powder blue Toyota Celica. She took me on one of my first trips to Reno. We are still close to this very day. We have been there for one another through some of the best times and the worst times. When her mother was diagnosed with cancer, she cried on my floor. When she left her relationship, she moved in with me. When my brother became ill, she was a listening ear for me. When her mother died, I was there for her. When my mother passed, she dropped everything to be there for me. She was my maid of honor at my wedding. She spoke at my father's funeral. She is no-nonsense. She tells me the truth. I am incredibly happy that I have a friend like her in my life.

As iron sharpens iron, so one person sharpens another.
Proverbs 27:17

When I was 17 years old, my dad, my mom and I were homeless. My mom was put in a convalescent hospital. I was sent to live with my aunt and uncle and my dad went to live with a friend and her three boys. My dad found us a house and on New Year's Day, we moved in with no furniture. I was so happy to be back with my family. We got my mom out of the hospital and we began to rebuild. As soon as I had gotten comfortable with my newfound happiness, my dad's friend and her three boys that he had been living with came knocking on our door, needing a place to stay. I hated the idea because it took my dad away from focusing on my mom and me. I wanted it to be just my family. Now we had 4 other people to deal with. Things were ok in the beginning, but they soon went downhill. The stench of three boys was so strong in the house that it made me sick, and they were always so loud.

My grandmother had died, and my dad went to Mississippi for her funeral. While he was gone, his friend and her kids were supposed to stay with me and help me take care of my mom but, that was never to be, they left as soon as my dad left. My mom had a seizure. I called my brother and the ambulance. The woman that had been staying with us had forgotten to give my mother her medicine. I was so angry because the blame was put on me. My dad was miles away, so he did not know what was going on. He thought I had told the woman to leave. He was more concerned with her and her family than what was going on with his wife and his child. I tried to tell my brother that I had some strange feelings about the woman, but he did not understand because he did not live with us. When my dad came back home, the woman and her kids came back. I was so angry that they came back after my mom's seizure. I ran out of the house and slammed the door. Thank goodness, just as I walked out of the door, my brother was pulling up in his green 1979 Camaro. I jumped in his car and told him to drive. He took me to his house, and he let me vent. I told him I did not want to stay there anymore. He took me back and when my dad tried to talk to me, I entered my room and slammed the door. My brother tried to talk to me too, but he got frustrated and walked out. At that time, I felt like I was all alone. No one understood me. My heart was broken into pieces. There was no one willing to listen to my concerns. I locked my door and cried myself to sleep.

I woke up the next day to a good friend from high school calling me. She was coming to my side of town and wanted to know if I wanted to hang out with her. I jumped at the chance. When she picked me up, she knew something was wrong. She could see it in my eyes. She had her little cousins and her boyfriend with her, so we could not talk much. After the night was over, she took me back home. Later that night, I got into an argument with my dad. I called my friend, and she came to pick me up the next day. I spent the weekend at her house. I explained everything. I left nothing out. I told her about my dad's relationship with the other woman. I told her how alone I felt. I told her I did not want to go back to my dad's house. I did not expect what happened next. She asked her mom if I could stay with her and her mom said yes. I was shocked. The next day we went to my dad's house in her gold Volkswagen bug and packed all my stuff. As we drove away, I felt the relief in my body like a balloon losing air from a tiny hole. I could breathe again.

My friend speaks for me, while my eyes pour out tears to God. He speaks to God for me, like someone presenting an argument for a friend. Job 16:20-21 ERV

I moved in with my friend and her mother. My dad and I did not talk for months. My aunt called me and told me that my dad wanted to talk to me. I finally let him talk to me, but I did not go back home. I stayed with my friend and her family for 5 years. We became a family. I called her mother "Madre." They saved my life. I had no clue what I would have done if I had not gone to stay with them. My dad was dealing with a lot at that time. I felt so sorry for my mom, but I had to save myself. I enjoyed living with my new family. I became an adult while living with them. I was in college, living my life and working. I was finally making my way into adulthood. It was a shock to my system when my dad called my job and asked to speak with me. Over the phone, he spoke the words, "Your brother is dead." I screamed at the top of my lungs in my office building. I grabbed my keys and rushed out of the office. My boss grabbed the phone and talked with my dad and ran after me. She ended up taking me home because she said I was in no condition to drive.

I was numb. My brother was the one person that had gone through everything with me. Now he was gone. I felt that I needed to be back with my family during that time, so I went back to my Madre's house, packed my bags, and left the key on the counter. I thought for sure that they would understand why I had to leave. I told them how I was feeling during that time but leaving the key on the counter became the ultimate wrong move.

I was lost for a while. It took several months for me to get back to some sense of normalcy. My brother passed in November and by the new year, my friend and Madre had invited me over for a get together. I went, but the feeling of family was off. As we set our goals for the year and discussed life, things just seemed different. I told them I had decided to move in with a friend from college. They were surprised. They did not come out and say it, but I knew that they were disappointed. The elephant stayed in the room that night; nothing got resolved.

The next time I saw my friend and Madre was the following New Year's Eve. Although we had a good time, there was a distance between my friend and me. We were not as close. In my mind, I had dealt with a lot of loss, hurt, and pain. I expected her to be understanding. The fact that we never discussed the way I left her house forged a large wall to build between us. I felt like there was a huge elephant in the room that suffocated the space whenever we were in it. Several years passed and she was getting married. I realized how big the elephant was when she did not allow me to be a part of her wedding. This was a big blow to my heart. I was devastated. She said that she felt that I was going through so much during that time that she did not think I could handle being in her wedding. She gave me no opportunity to choose. I still went to her wedding. I smiled and said nice things, but I was hurt. I watched as women I did not know walked down the aisle in their soft off-white gowns. I knew I should have been walking down the aisle instead of them.

Years later, we had a long talk about that period. She told me that her mother felt disrespected by the way I left the key on the counter. I had gone through something so tragic that I did not know how to feel and what to do. I only knew I needed to be with my mom and dad at the time. I did not think it was wrong at all. I thought they would understand my plight. I never knew Madre and my friend took things so hard. I was proud of the fact that we could sit down and talk things out as adults and forgive one another for our miscommunication.

> **"Let no corrupting talk come out of your mouths, but only such as is good for building up, as fits the occasion, that it may give grace to those who hear." Ephesians 4:29**

My friend was always there for me during those hard moments. During my father's last days, she showed up for both of us. We were not expecting her at the hospital. She held my dad's hand and played Marvin Sapp on her phone. My dad cried out he was not afraid to die.

My dad called her his angel. She showed up once again right on time as an angel in disguise.

For he will command his angels concerning you to guard you in all your ways-Psalms 91:11.

To this day, we talk about how we have always been there for one another. Through all the ups and downs of our friendship, she became more than a friend to me. She became my sister. I would not have it any other way. Sometimes, we must have difficult conversations to clear up the miscommunication. I was able to have a difficult conversation with Madre as well. I was able to tell her that she did not have to allow me to move in with her and her daughter, but I was so grateful that she did. I learned so much from being in her house during that time. I learned how to be a strong woman by watching Madre. She worked, went to school, and owned her house. I was amazed at the way she handled everything. Watching her do that allowed me to see that I could do that too. I told her that she helped me become the woman that I am today, and I love her for it. My friend and I continue to have those deep conversations. She is someone that I truly trust with my life. She showed me what true sisterhood is and I am grateful to have her in my life.

Another friendship that I have had for the same number of years showed me how to let the past stay in the past. This friend and I always had fun times together. In the ninth grade, when we met, she was a cheerleader. At the end of the school year, we had decided to try out for the song squad together. We worked on our routine and had fun putting it together. We tried out and she became the leader for the song squad for the next year. My name was not on the list. I was hurt. I wanted to be a part of the squad. I thought if I made the squad, it would keep my dad from moving us to another area of the city. He made us move that summer, so I started a new school the following school year. I hated that I had to move away from my friends. My friend's mother surprised her daughter by picking me up and bringing me to spend the night for my friend's birthday weekend that August. That night, my friend and I plotted a way for me to stay with her and her family for the next school year so that I did not have to change schools. Of course, that plan did not work. I had a good time that weekend, but I had to go back to my new location to start my high school sophomore year. Thankfully, my friend and I kept in contact and we got together often.

Over the years, this friend and I talked on the phone for hours at a time. It was our thing. We would discuss life, movies, and song lyrics. When we started college, she became a mom. I loved spending time with her little boy. He had so much energy. Around that time, my brother had a little girl that I fell in love with immediately. My niece and I would hang out with my friend and her son often. When her son became an adult, he asked to borrow my car. I allowed him to and of course, he had an accident. I was disappointed in the way the situation was handled. She advised me that I had to deal with her son directly regarding my car. She would not have any part in the discussion. It ruined the friendship. We did not talk for several years. Unfortunately, it took her brother's death to bring us back together. She called me to let me know that he had died. I immediately let the situation between us go and was by her side in her time of need. We were able to repair our friendship and we are friends today. It was horrible that it took a death to repair our relationship. I was there for her when she needed me the same way she had been there for me. We had something in common. We had both lost a sibling. The pain and grief that is felt in that situation is like no other. I was proud to be there for her and help her through that situation. I was able to show her that although the pain of the loss lasts forever, the way you deal with it changes with time.

As I stated at the top of my story, I have never had trouble meeting friends. I have always been able to be a good friend. This past year, I was able to meet a group of women that kept that going for me. I met Nakia Austin on Facebook while I was surfing the net. She was giving her testimony on Facebook live. The way she told her story captivated me. I wanted to know more about this woman. She was having a challenge online and I joined. I would listen to her daily as she talked about the word of God. She explained how she believed in His word and He helped heal her. I realized that I needed the healing that she talked about. She had a conference and due to COVID-19 it was transferred from a location in Ohio to online. I bought a ticket, and I was amazed at how Nakia and the other speakers opened my heart again to trust in God. The conference was amazing. The women of the conference prayed for me personally. Once it was over, I wanted more.

There was an opportunity to become an ambassador of 100 Healed. I decided to put in my application. I was chosen as an ambassador. I met the other ambassadors online and it was as if we had known one another all our lives. These women prayed for me. They laughed and cried with me. We easily built a sisterhood. We care about one another's well-being. We got the chance to meet one another in person this past October and it was an amazing time. Nakia knew what she was doing when she put us together. It was easy. We had no issues. We became a family.

As I talk about the situations that I have been through in my life, I could not imagine going through those hard times without my friends who have become my sisters. I believe that in every situation that I have been through; God has sent someone into my life that was the right person for that time. I treasure each of my friends for what they have brought to my life.

Sisterhood is especially important to me. I am proud to call the ladies in my life my sisters. We have all been there for one another through the ups and downs of life. Even when we thought that situations were bringing our friendships to an end, we found a way to bring things back together. You may feel like friendships with women are difficult, or you may have those relationships like mine that fill your heart with joy, either way, I pray that my story has given you new insight into how important sisterhood is.

I pray that you learn from my story; that it takes being open and vulnerable to have a true sisterhood. I used to be someone that kept my issues to myself. I did not think anyone would understand me.

Sometimes you must have hard conversations to build a relationship. Things can be difficult, but if you are willing to open up and share, you will have a sister for a lifetime.

My secret to sisterhood is to always be willing to have the hard conversations. Don't think about the conversation too much in your head before you talk because it could cause you to back pedal. If your sisters are true friends, they will be open to listen to you. You will both be able to voice your concerns and come out with a new understanding of one another. There is nothing that a good conversation can't solve.

Heavenly Father, I come before you giving you all the glory, the honor and praise for you are so worthy. I pray that the sister reading this story learns to be open and vulnerable with her friends. I hope she realizes that sometimes you must have hard conversations to build a relationship. Father give her the words to speak to clear up any confusion in any situation that comes her way. Let her know that things do get difficult from time to time but if she is willing to open up and share, she will have a sister for a lifetime. In Jesus' most precious name I pray,
Amen.

Sharice Porter *is an author of two book compilations "Breaking Through Barriers" and "Diary of a Ready Woman." She is also a speaker who wants to let young women know that they have everything they need inside of them to make their dreams come true. She has a message of faith and determination and hopes to reach young girls and women that feel hurt by what life has thrown at them. She wants to show them that even though they may have had rainy days in their past, a rainbow always shows up after the rain. She has come a long way by faith and works daily to realize that with GOD all things are possible to obtain. Through her books and motivational speaking her mission is to inspire and empower girls and women to understand that even though there may be some scars in life, with time scars do heal. She loves to write and travel. Some of her favorite destinations have been Egypt and Israel. To contact Sharice - Email: psharice@hotmail.com | Facebook.com/Sharice.Porter*

Chapter 2

My Heart is Safe With My Sisters

Maintaining Friendships Through Empathy and Emotional Honesty

By Bridgette Smith

I know we have heard rumors and negative talk about relationships among women, but I'm here to let you in on a little secret. Sisterhood is valuable and very important. **My secret to maintaining healthy relationships is to lead with empathy and be transparent with your emotions.** We all have a story, don't be afraid to share yours. Here's mine.

I'm an only child. I was born in the early 80's and lived in the home with my mother, grandmother, great-aunt and an older cousin who was also like a second mom. It was my great-grandmother's home, and she had an open-door policy. If our family needed somewhere to stay, they could always come to 2259 until they got back on their feet. Even after her passing, the open-door policy remained. Within the home, I saw a strong sisterhood. They worked together to pay the bills and prepare the meals. They loved and cared for each other and they all made sure I was taken care of. The value of having a tribe of women to help you throughout life is a lesson I learned early. Women who love you and want to see you thrive are vital. To be loved through your shortcomings and always having a place to call home is my greatest blessing.

I was raised in a cocoon of love and was sheltered. While my extended family was busy making sure I was well adjusted, my mom was slipping into addiction. Crack cocaine had hit our communities hard. It was no longer a "party drug" but had become a monster that was ruining families and destroying homes. My sisterhood tribe really stepped up. I was unaware of how the disease of addiction was crippling my mother. They didn't tell me what was going on for a few years. I only noticed that she was leaving home more and eventually moved out. My Grandmother, Great-aunt and cousin continued to care for me.

When I was 10 years old, my Uncle Roger, my mother's only sibling was murdered, and my grandmother died one month later. The grief of losing her brother and mother caused my mom to spiral further into addiction. As you can imagine, my life changed drastically at this time too. I was grieving my family's loss and all I wanted was for my mother to get better and come back home. I felt abandoned even with the love of my aunt and cousin. I was unable to see the blessing that this sisterhood had afforded me. I wasn't being thrust into the lifestyle of having an addict as a parent; I was safe. My needs were met; you could even say I was spoiled. My Auntie always says " you aren't spoiled bae you are well loved." My entire family poured into me and overcompensated for my mother's shortcomings. Eventually, this would shape who I was going to become within my friendships. I became "the savior". When my friends had a problem, I was swooping in to save the day. I tried to solve problems from what I thought I would need in a situation without really stopping to ask them what they needed from me. However, when I needed help and they didn't respond to me like I thought they should, it built up resentment in me. On my quest for healing and self-love, I have learned that my resentments were from my own expectations. I want to share with you how self-love and empathy will help you maintain stronger relationships with your sister-friends.

Webster's dictionary defines empathy as the action of understanding, being aware of, being sensitive to, and vicariously experiencing the feelings, thoughts, and experience of another of either the past or present without having the feelings, thoughts, and experience fully communicated in an objectively explicit manner also: the capacity for this. The Bible says in Romans 12:15 "Rejoice with those that rejoice, and weep with those who weep". Be emotionally available and present with your sisters.

I met my first bestie in the 2nd grade, but we became sisters in the

6th grade. She was outgoing and adventurous. She came into my life like a ball of light. She was the distraction I needed. We reconnected when we were sent to the same middle school and had the same bus stop. She was an only child, just like me and she lived right around the corner. I could see her house from my backyard. While I was quiet and reserved, she was the jokester and quickly pulled me out of my shell. While I wanted to stay in my room and read a book, she wanted to hang out outside. We were in honors classes, but she made being a nerd cool. We spent all our time together. She seemed never to want to go home. We navigated some big milestones together, starting our cycles, getting our first bra and of course, crushes. We grew very close, but I was embarrassed about my mom's addiction and I didn't tell her about it for many years. While I was being emotionally supportive for her, I didn't allow her the opportunity to be there for me. From her point of view, she thought I had it made. I had my own room, with cable, my own phone line, and I wasn't monitored with the music I listened to. My great-aunt didn't talk loud or curse at me. Her home was much different. She was monitored heavily on what she could wear, the movies she could watch, and it was common to be called out of your name in casual conversation by the women in her family. She found solitude at my house and she spent a ton of time there with me. I didn't know how to tell her that I would give all this up for my mom to be sober. I didn't want to come off as ungrateful. As a child, I didn't realize that my family's empathy for my mother is what ultimately saved me from the horrors that so many have gone through due to having parents that used drugs.

The summer before she and I became sisters, my mom had been released from prison and she and my father were back together. We would spend the weekends with my parents at my father's home. My sister's love for my mom and dad made me look at them in a different light. As I viewed them from a lens of disappointment and heartbreak due to their lifestyle choices, she saw the fun and easy-going nature of them. At first, I was annoyed at her attachment to my mother. I would find her and my mother lounging together watching lifetime movies and eating snacks and I would think to myself, "whose company, are you?" Looking back, seeing her enjoy my mom's company made me want to forgive her and spend time with her too. My sister coming into my life when she did was God's gift to me to be able to love my parents past my expectations of them. To be thankful for the life that my aunt and cousin provided me and instead of fighting to be with my parents full time I realized that I could enjoy them on the weekends and get them at their best during that time. They still struggled with addiction during this time, and I was emotionally affected by it, but I never told my friend how I was feeling. I was emotionally dishonest.

It took me years to really express how deeply I was hurting but once I opened up to her, I can still see her shocked expression and tear-filled eyes when my sister embraced me. The embarrassment and worry I felt was all for nothing. She still loved me and embraced just like a sister should. The relief I felt was indescribable. We have been sisters for almost 30 years now and have been able to support each other through all our greatest accomplishments, marriage, children, and graduations and also our lowest points as well. Through it all I know that my heart is safe with my sister.

I lost my father to sclerosis of the liver in 2018. All my best memories include my parents, myself, and my sister. With being an only child and losing a parent, I can call my sister on those days when I'm missing him or even mad at him for dying and she will remind me of a memory of us and after the tears, we are usually cracking up. That part of this sisterhood is priceless and a great treasure. We have had our share of disagreements over the years, but the empathy we have for one another helps us to forgive each other. How do you break up with your sister anyway, right?

I met my second sister on the first day of 7th grade. I had been transferred to another school because my grades had dropped. I was busy hanging with my friends and talking on the phone. It left little time to study. My aunt thought it would be best to give me more structure by sending me to a Christian-based school. On the ride to school, an argument began and the girl in the seat next to me was trying to lunge over the seat to hit the girl she was arguing with! I grabbed her and pulled her back down into the seat and whispered to her, "You know your mama is going to kill you if you get suspended and we haven't made it through the first day of school." She became very still and looked at me and was like, "you are right" we both shared a laugh and introduced ourselves.

I guess I don't have to tell you this, but she was a fighter. I spent the beginning of our sisterhood talking her out of fighting and solving her problems in ways that did not include her being suspended or arrested. She lived in the home with her mother and 2 brothers. Her mother was a nurse and worked nights, so she spent a lot of time unsupervised. She could drive when she was 15 and often picked me up in her mother's car. She was very mature, and my aunt barely wanted me off the front porch, trusted that I was in good hands when I was with her and I was. She always made sure I was safe and felt comfortable. When we were sixteen, she gave birth to her first son and named me his Godmother. I was honored and took that role very seriously. She was a single mom and I wanted to make sure that I was there for her and helped her financially.

Once I graduated from high school, I went out of state to college. I didn't realize it at the time, but she felt abandoned by me. After graduation, I moved back home, and she now had 3 sons. We were navigating through life completely different, but I valued her friendship. I didn't know how to support her. I had majored in psychology and I knew that trying to save people from their problems was me avoiding my own issues. I had no idea how to maintain our relationship because I did not have the resources to make her life easier and give her an escape as I had when we were kids. Instead, we started having coffee dates. We would meet and give each other a chance to really talk about our struggles. I talked about my mother's addiction; she talked about her mother being emotionally unavailable. That was the first time that I heard, "I didn't know you felt like that about your mom; you were always so happy." Again, I had been emotionally shut down from my sister. I offered empathy to my sisters but had not allowed them in so they could return that gift to me. In my attempt to be perfect and a good daughter to be enough for my mother to stop doing drugs, I was masking the turmoil that my heart was really feeling.

She really helped me work through some tough feelings, and I supported her as she navigated being a single mom. I was her greatest cheerleader and the way my family poured into me I made it my mission to do the same for my sister. I was by her side at the boys' sports events and my Godson's graduation. She calls me her therapist. She's my diary. I know that I can tell her all my secrets and they are safe with her. It's a judgement free zone.

My sister and I are navigating a storm together now. My Godson is battling a terminal illness. I know that just being there to support her emotionally is what I am being called to do. It could have been God's reason for me to intervene on the day we met. While I thought that financial support was the most important thing I could provide when we were younger, I now understand that someone in your corner and holding your hand through hard times is what counts the most. Having a friend that will let you weep when your heart is broken and loving you back to wholeness even when it doesn't seem possible is what sisterhood is about.

I was invited to a healing retreat in 2019 by the leader of 100 Healed, Nakia Austin. I had lost my father and was sitting with all those old feelings of disappointment and anger of the lifestyle that he chose that led him to an early demise. When she in boxed me, I didn't think I was dealing with trauma. She asked me a series of questions and I indeed was traumatized. I showed up scared. She made it clear that this was a working retreat; it would require emotional honesty and the willingness to express our hurts but also to take accountability for how we respond to them. I couldn't deflect like I was used to doing while helping others. I had to unpack my neatly packed hurts and allow my sisters to support me. The Divine 9 was what we were dubbed. In 3 days, we became a family and the burdens I had been carrying for 30 years seemed to dissipate. Have you asked for help? Have you told anyone how they can support you? Those 2 questions caused so many tears because I had not. I was walking around hurting and exhausting myself, so I wouldn't burden anyone, and it was destroying me. Can you look at your life and see how your sisters can support you? Are you willing to just ask them for help?

Through my personal journey of healing and self-love, I was honored to be called to be an Ambassador for 100 Healed. Being involved with a group of women who pray for each other and who offer a safe space where I can take off my cape and be vulnerable and not feel like it's my job to make the world turn is what I needed. Having daily reminders that I am loved and important and I don't have to do anything to deserve it because it's coming directly from God through my sisters is healing. We are all on a quest to let go of past hurts and traumas and we touch and agree that it's possible to fully heal and not just get over our heartaches. It was because of our past that we would be able to help other sisters heal and be accountable for one another. 1 Peter 4:8-10 says, "Above all, keep loving one another earnestly. Since love covers a multitude of sins. Be hospitable to one another without grumbling. As each one has received a gift, minister it to one another as good stewards of the manifold grace of God. Offer empathy, grace, and love for your fellow sisters. We all have a story. Practice putting yourself in another's shoes. Listen with an open heart, and above all, be emotionally honest.

My prayer is that your sisters are always there to support you with kind words, loving correction, prayer, and positive affirmations. I pray that you find the courage to be emotionally honest and brave enough to ask for help. If you have not found your sisterhood, please join us on Facebook at Awaken! It is our mission to love and support you through your healing journey.

Dear God, I come to you with an open heart. Allow me to lead with your loving grace and kindness. Allow me to see my sisters through your eyes. Remind me that we are all a manifestation of your divine love and we need each other to survive even when we are in a disagreement. Let me be slow to anger and quick to forgive. Let me also see the value in our differences as we need them to grow. Continue to order our steps so our lives can be pleasing to you. In your precious son's name.

Amen.

Bridgette Smith is a wife and mother of 3 beautiful children and bonus mom to twin stepsons. She is a proud graduate of Tennessee State University. She is an ambassador of the 100 Healed movement that is dedicated to women healing from trauma and cultivating a stronger sisterhood.

To contact Bridgette - Facebook.com/bridgette.green.16 | Instagram: @prettypisces_312

Chapter 3

Embracing Who You Are
Misunderstandings and Jealousy
By Charity Todd

In this world many things are superficial, shallow, and empty. With so many new and exciting technological advances and ways of communicating, we have forgotten the most important and effective ways to communicate, which is a simple face to face or a phone call. And because of that most of our relationships lack real depth. We no longer take the time to really get to know one another and build lasting lifelong relationships.

If one is blessed and fortunate enough to have sister-friends either biologically or united by life's experiences, know that experience is invaluable. I have recently become part of a sisterhood. I now have friends that I did not know I needed! I have found this to be an irreplaceable experience! Such a sense of belonging, love, and support. A safe place just to be myself. My sisters have proven to be a lifeline for me during an exceedingly difficult and challenging time in my life. I truly value and appreciate all my sisters and I will cherish this experience for the rest of my life!

Since it is possible to have this type of connection and bond between women, especially those who are not related to one another, how did we coin the phrase "Women cannot be friends?" How do we end up with catty petty squabbles in the workplace? Why can't women get along? Are there secrets to having a healthy sisterhood? Why are we jealous of one another?

I have learned that jealousy, envy and competing with one another will quickly destroy all friendships and relationships especially the relationship you have with your sisters. Have you ever stopped to ask yourself, am I jealous of her and why? How do we find ourselves comparing our lives and accomplishments? Why do we try to get the boss to notice us and congratulate us in front of our female coworkers? We even break out our family pictures to show off our family's beauty and achievements. It is not just to share and be proud, but to show that my family is better than yours.

Jealousy can lead to bitterness, envy, discontentment, anxiety, and depression. It is an unseen enemy that desires to make you feel inadequate, unworthy, and not good enough. If James 3:16 says, "For where you have envy and selfish ambition, there you will find disorder and every evil practice". And "If you bite and devour each other, watch out you will be destroyed by each other" (Galatians 5:15), there must be a reason why women fall into jealousy and competition.

My secret to sisterhood is learning and embracing who you are.
I am one of five children, the middle child having one sister and three brothers. I have always desired to have female friends- a tribe if you will. Coming from a moderate size family you just get used to having people around. It was not until my sister and I were adults that I understood how I truly undervalued the importance of having a sister. I did not realize that she was my 1st friend, my only friend. With five children in the home, we did not visit others too often.

Technically my sister is 11 months older than me, which means for about a week every year we are the same age! #Twinning has been our thing every birthday month, how awesome is that! We had no history of fighting or disagreements that I can recall, but something was missing. Reflecting, I remember this longing to be accepted. I wanted my own friends! Sounds childish but when you always share everything it is nice when you have things that are just for you.

Memory #1:
I can remember on two occasions that I thought I had kind of connected with other females thinking I have found myself a friend only to find out we were cool, but they had befriended someone very close to me, my sister.

No worries, don't be petty I would tell myself but, why is this still on my mind, why does this bother me? Why does this hurt? I am a strong black female, business owner, entrepreneur, wife, and mother hear me ROAR! These memories have stirred up something inside of me causing me to ask questions about who I am. Did they not like me? Did I say something, do something that would cause these individuals to not want to develop a closer friendship? I almost forgot "Women cannot be friends" why am I trippin'?

Looking back, it seems like every time I had opened myself up to befriend someone thinking ok, she is cool, I can see us becoming great friends, it did not happen. We may have similar experiences even like the same things, be around the same age and have many similarities! I do not understand why it is so hard to find a good female friend.

Who needs friends when you have family? Back to the memory, I recall being super excited to meet a new cousin. She was just a year older than me, fun personality and we got along great. I am not sure when she and my sister started hanging but it was ok because we are family. I noticed she no longer called me, but she would call my sister. As time went on, we just stopped speaking altogether. I do not really know the reason why. She had just graduated high school. Perhaps we just grew apart because she is grown and going off to college. Girl do not be immature. One day I heard my sister on the phone making plans to go visit her. Wow, have they maintained communication this whole time? It sounded as if they had become the best of friends. Girl stop being petty, are you jealous of their friendship? Maybe they just had more in common, maybe she liked your sister better. Life goes on.

I met another potential friend. Her personality was a bit much, but she was cool. She was a little younger than me, but I thought it could work. We were both young and married to older men. It is important to have like- minded people in your life that understand where you are coming from. I was at a place in my life where I really needed someone (other than family) to talk to. We did live in 2 different states, which was fine. When we saw each other, she would encourage me with just a look. She understood my pain and I understood hers.

Wait what just happened? How? When? I am not with my sister 24/7 but when did they become the best of friends? One day we were visiting, and it was apparent that they had become the best of friends! I feel petty for even mentioning it, but it really bothered me.

Now I am in my thoughts, what is wrong with me? Am I not likeable? Was I offensive in some way? What is it? Over the years I have struggled immensely in this area of maintaining friendships. It must be me! I mean, I have been told I am arrogant, high minded, selfish, and mean. Uncaring, unsupportive, and condescending. Wow! These words are intense. Maybe this is the reason I do not connect with others on a deeper level. Is there any truth to these harsh words?

Let us take a moment and talk about this. I am remembering this experience that I had several years ago like it was yesterday, and it was not very pleasant. It seems a bit misplaced to mention on my journey to understand why women find it hard to become friends, but it may shed some light into my personal journey to understand me and who I am.

Memory #2
I remember being pulled into a meeting with two individuals that wanted to tell me all the things they did not like about me. They read off about two pages each, front and back! What is this? High school? They thought I was not considerate of them and their feelings, unsupportive and high minded. I was in a position of authority and at times had to instruct and critique. Leading is not an easy job however I took my responsibilities very seriously. When you are in a leadership position, there are times when you must make recommendations, and keep order. Sometimes telling a person what they do not want to hear, comes with the territory.

How could I have been so misunderstood? I do not remember being malicious in my delivery, nevertheless it was perceived that way. However, wrong, or malicious that meeting felt to me, I asked myself was there any truth to it? You do have a bad track record when it comes to maintaining friendships, maybe I need to be more like others. At the time all I felt was anger for the individuals who had "plotted" against me. They also told untruths about me in that particular "meeting". However, that was their perspective and their experience of me. How could I have been so misunderstood? Was there any truth to what they said or felt? What type of vibe was I giving off that was so offensive to them? I was unconscious and unaware of how I related to others at this time in my life. Where did this come from? I think I decided this day to no longer be open to new friendships. If I cannot be me, I would rather just stay to myself. I stopped speaking my opinions with certain individuals, just kind of stayed to myself thinking this is safer. Speaking my mind has not served me well in the past. So, I thought, if I were more like so and so, if I had a bubblier personality maybe these kinds of experiences would not happen.

Memory #3

Church was awesome today! We were getting ready to leave and the pastor at that time said to me "You sing good, but your sister! Whew. She can really SANG!" He reiterates, "You can sing, but not like your sister". I nodded and smiled. I do not remember crying at that moment. I think anger and jealousy for my sister's singing ability entered my heart that day. Here I am singing my heart out before God and my pastor compares me to my sister. He could not have known how those words cut through me and still at times haunt me even to this very day. I remember thinking, "she is better than me and always has been". Going to the same high school as siblings and relatives I remember hearing the words, "Oh you're not like your sister".

They had no idea of the impact of their words. I believe the feelings of not feeling good enough stemmed from this moment. What is it that she has that I do not? Did I allow someone to place this unhealthy spirit of jealousy, which led to competition on me? I started trying to model myself after her and her singing ability. Almost going horse trying to imitate her style of singing. Then of course I would try to mimic other singers, every note every musical run they did, not to learn how but, just to sound like them since that is what I thought the people desired.

I love my sister dearly, how did I let this happen? She is not my competition. Looking back, I believe I felt insecure, and I allowed others' opinions of me to plague my mind. I allowed someone to compare our God given gifts against each other. My reply should have been yes, she is amazing but guess what I am amazing too. I felt in that moment that I needed to mimic and become just like her because of someone else's opinion.

I believe that from these experiences I have felt the need to prove myself. Who I was and what I had to offer wasn't enough? Looking back, I remember feeling inadequate, defective, less than capable. I wondered, what is my character lacking? I became jealous of others ability to get along well with everyone. I was envious of personality traits or talents that I saw in others. From these and other moments like these in my life I have never been my true self because I thought there was something wrong with my true authentic self. When I was just being me, I was most offensive to others. Very misunderstood.
I believe that every experience in life, whether it is good or bad, shapes you into who you are. I believe more than ever seeds of jealousy were sown into my life without my permission, but I did not realize how much it affected me until adulthood. I also am realizing some of the not so pleasant encounters had me pull back from even wanting to pursue friendships with others. I do not ever want to feel again like I did growing up, thinking something was wrong with me or that I am not likable or worthy of real genuine sister friends and I never want to be offensive to others.

So now what? Now that I understand more about who I am. I did lack self-esteem and confidence in some areas. I have come to understand (through counseling) that I do have a strong personality. I am very direct, and this characteristic is not for everybody. That does not have to be a negative. I just needed to know who I am; Opinionated, passionate, talented, plain spoken and just unique!

I believe, knowing who you are is most important before finding your tribe. Being confident and comfortable with yourself will show you who you will best resonate with. I thought I needed to change to fit in with other crowds. No, do not change yourself to fit another model, be your own model! I believe your tribe will be drawn to you! Friends that best match you and your ideas and thought processes. Everyone that comes in your life has a purpose, however, everyone is not meant to stay in your life forever. Some friendships are seasonal. That too does not have to be a negative. The time has just expired on what purpose they were meant for in your life. Ecclesiastes 3:1 says there is a time for everything. There is a season for everything and a time for every delight and event or purpose under heaven. This scripture has had a tremendous impact on how I now see things! Timing is everything! Understanding where each of us are in our lives and understanding what we need or do not need is imperative.

I understand now very clearly that I have been carrying around all my past experiences, internalizing them and little by little they became a part of me. "Hurt People Hurt People" whether knowingly or unknowingly and unintentionally. Since I "had" to change me to be more acceptable, likable, I held others to that same standard. Clearly this was not a good idea.

Before dismissing friends from your inner circle, understand this, we all need something different. We are all different and it is those differences that make us all special. Embracing our differences is such a simple but invaluable piece of advice that I have learned from my sister-friends.

When you are ready and open to new friends ask yourself a few questions first. Are you in need of someone who will hold you accountable or hold you to a higher standard? Friends that will share and support your ideas, life goals and business ventures? Knowing what you need or want out of a friendship is extremely important. Do you require a lot of one-on-one time? Do you need to talk every day or occasionally? If you are a little clingier you will not match well with a person who is not. They may seem callous or cold to you but perfect for another person. And it is ok to have more than one friend circle. You need to simply understand who you are and what you are looking for.

Be open to meeting new friends. There may be a coworker that is just that but given an opportunity she may have a lot in common with you and this just might turn into a beautiful friendship.
There is a level of being vulnerable or letting your guard down a little, (while using discernment) that may be difficult because sometimes we have put walls up due to the bad life experiences we have had. If we do not let people in, we will miss wonderful life opportunities because of past hurts and disappointments.

Seek therapy, there are times when we just need to talk and dig into our past to unlock and heal any old wounds you may have. You do not want to carry around that baggage. It will ruin your potential friendships and relationships with others.

Build your faith. If there is brokenness in your life on a level that no one understands perhaps there is a spiritual issue or concern that needs addressing. I will take this moment to encourage you and to let you know that God loves you more than anyone in the world could ever love you. It does not matter where your decisions in life have taken you, God loves you still. It does not matter what you did yesterday, Jesus died just for YOU! John 3:16 says, For God so loved the world that he gave His only son, that whoever believes in Him should not perish but have eternal life. God longs to be your friend. I'm reminded of a song that some of the lyrics say "Friend, there will never be a friend as dear to me as you there will never be another closer than a brother. He is always worth the wait, faithful as the day, you say we are friends". When you feel alone, know that God is always there, a true friend. He is concerned about you and wants to see you live a life fulfilled. He came so that you might have an abundant life. Full of joy, success, and happiness! You are uniquely created, fearfully, remarkably, and wonderfully made! You are awesome! Your life has purpose!

Remember failed friendships of the past are simply that, in the past.

Do not stay there, learn from your mistakes, and embrace who you are.

Women can be friends! It was not until I met a group of ladies, took a leap of faith, and became vulnerable with these thoughts and feelings that I feel that I have found my tribe. It has taken about a year to fully trust and know that they are real and genuine. These ladies are most loving and supportive. I do not feel a need to compete, mimic or try to be like anyone. I do not feel inferior in fact, I feel more empowered every time we meet.

One of my secrets of sisterhood is to embrace one another's differences, not to be jealous or envious of them. Celebrate each other's accomplishments. I am so grateful for the women God has placed in my life, past present and future!

Heavenly Father, I pray that everyone who reads this book be encouraged and know that they are not alone. Lord, you are faithful to forgive our sins and past mistakes and shortcomings. We lay our burdens at your feet and cast all our cares on you. Lord, I pray every person who reads this will feel your love today. This we pray in Jesus mighty name,
Amen!

Charity Todd, *is a wife and a mother of 6 beautiful children. Two biological and four bonus blessings. At the age of 12, she decided to pursue a career in Cosmetology and made sure she met this goal. Currently, Charity has a successful growing salon and desires to give back to her community with employment opportunities for others who desire to work in this field. While operating in the business world, Charity is also an active member in her church and loves to help others.*

Although a first time author, Charity desires to write more books sharing the highs and lows of becoming who you are. With an amazing husband and family by her side, Charity understands and believes, that the sky truly is the limit to what you can have. You are what you think!
To contact Charity - Email: rosi3t@icloud.com | Instagram: @ hairconfidencesalon

Chapter 4

Be Authentically You

By Stephanie Cherise Bell

My secret sauce to sisterhood is to authentically be you! How many of us have said "just do you?" I think at one point in my life this was my favorite saying. I would say it with the thought that I was never going to in life let anyone be close to me. I felt friendship was fake. I felt like people could only love me to the point of what I could do for them and once the trajectory of what I could do changed then everything else changed. I believe that at one point I hated anything to do with love so that also included friendship. I was done with it all. I made a conscious decision that I was my own best friend even though I really did not even like being my own friend. I realized my attitude about friendship and about life was coming from a place of nothing but pain. I was my own problem. I am not saying that the things that I went through were all my fault, but I was the common denominator for many of the repeated issues I went through. This was truly a result of how I looked at myself. How I saw myself. I was reminded of a scripture in 1 Samuel 16:7:

But the LORD said unto Samuel, look not on his countenance, or on the height of his stature; because I have refused him: for [the LORD seeth] not as man seeth; for man looketh on the outward appearance, but the LORD looketh on the heart.

When I first read this scripture, I thought to myself "Why have you been tripping all these years? I do not love myself, shoot I do not even like me." It took 50 years for me to figure out that I have set myself up in every friendship to fail because I did not authentically look at the dynamics of who I was on the inside to see who other people were. I viewed my appearance as less than anything that God's eyes could have seen for me. I did not focus on what my heart had to offer or feel.

I focused more on what I could give or how I could help.

Let me explain how I really saw myself. Well, first and foremost I looked at how I was taught at such a young age to believe who my family said I was. I would see myself as overweight, not smart, incomplete, co-dependent, ugly you name it that is who I was. The circumstances in my life added to my thoughts of feeling incomplete because I could not have kids. I was raped. I have a scar on my face and my feet are dislocated. I had the need to be needed. I internalized everything for years. I was habitually self-sabotaging myself. I asked myself, "what can I do to overcompensate for all of the flaws that are weighing me down on the outside.?" "How could I make someone see that I have a true heart to give and to love.?" I was consumed with my sad story that went back to childhood. In my mind I thought my mom hates me. I never felt deserving of her love. I still ask myself, was it about me? What caused me to be afraid of having friendships or getting close to anyone? Functioning friendships for me were only if I could keep the friendship centered around what my friends were dealing with and how I could help them be ok. It was never anything to do with how I felt.

What did this way of thinking do for me? Nothing, but left me feeling tired, unloved, unwanted, and taken advantage of and never understood. How could someone get who I was when I was never forthcoming with who I was on the inside. I never explained where my heart to love unconditionally or the desire to give came from. This was my true nature so in all honesty I never felt I needed to explain it. I never let anyone close to me. I never let anyone in to talk about all the pain from my past. I never shared how the way I saw myself was hurting me so much. I did not think sharing my feelings with a family member, or friend or doctor could really help with what I was going through. I should have shared how I wanted to have the love in return that I gave to the world. The love that I longed for did not happen for me the way I expected so I became angry. How could I possibly feel disappointed in someone that never ever knew who I was? How could I be upset and feel like people just used me for what I could do for them when I allowed things to happen this way? I had to realize that looking at my outer appearance did nothing for me but allowed what I considered my flaws to show up every time I looked in the mirror. It caused me to pretend to be something to everyone that I am not. I began to slip into a place where I began to recreate and repeat the same scenarios. Everything now became a lie.

There is no way I can be mad at the people I set up to love me based on a false sense of perception. The same way I was taught to see myself is the same way I am teaching others to see me. This is not easy to talk about but to be a real friend and enjoy the benefits of sisterhood you must allow your heart to be open and you must be yourself. You must be honest. You will find yourself at 50 years old talking and reliving the rape you had at 18 as if it were two weeks ago. Talk about being bi-polar! I kept saying, "Why did they do that to me?" 32 years later I was crying like it just happened, yesterday. Reflections hurt but when you have allowed yourself to be open and honest with others by sharing your story you become vulnerable to living it repeatedly. It would have been easier to share my story when the topic came up in conversation. I did not share my heart with my friends for fear of being judged or shamed by them. My friends would always ask "Why are you tripping?" In my mind I would start sharing all the details of my youth and adult life that I was afraid to be open about. I would share with them how my mom treated me differently from my sisters. How I never felt like I fit in with any of my family. How when I got married my husband even put me down saying if I left him, I would never find another man to love me. I would share how he spit in my face with all the might in his body. I wanted my friends to know. I wanted my family to know what I went through. I shared it all in my head, but the words never came out of my mouth. I did not know how to share what I had been through verbally. I wanted to share how I felt about myself, but I never did.

The hardest part about all of this was every time something happened with my friends, a misunderstanding was sure to follow. It would cause me to shut down and act as if I did not care. I would pretend that they meant nothing to me. That is when I adopted the phrase "Do you." Deep down I really cared. I wanted to call and say something.

I wanted to ask for clarity or apologize. I always felt like I really could not make that call or have a true deep conversation because I did not feel like I had a voice. The misunderstandings always left me back at square one. Another piece to suppress. The feelings of rejection and abandonment showed up a lot in my life. It reached the point where I thought," Why live?" I felt like people really did not care about me. Suicidal thoughts were always an easy route for me. It was so hard for me to say how I felt. I felt weak. I could never express that to anyone.

I am now learning to no longer be afraid to see myself as God sees me. He sees my heart. Seeing myself the way God sees me changed me and made a difference in my life. The bible says in Psalm 37:4 says, "Take delight in the Lord, and he will give you the desires of your heart." Taking delight in the Lord means that our hearts will truly find peace, love, and complete fulfillment in the God we serve. If we genuinely want what our heart is longing for then this type of satisfaction and worth will only come in a relationship with Christ. A life of pretense only leaves you continuously searching for more and more love outside of yourself.

I always felt that there was something different about the way I loved to give love away. I mean with no hesitation, no regret not one second thought towards the task at hand. If I could help, I wanted to do just that. It did not matter how sincere I was in this area; I had no personal substance to add to it. How many of you are familiar with church? I went to a church where I felt the self-discovery begin. I found a place where I could really cry out. No one knew why I was crying. That is what church folks do, especially in the Church of God in Christ... they cry. I will never forget my first experience. I was so scared. I grew up going to church where the church bus or van picked me up for children's church. It was an all-white church. We sang hymnals. We also went to church camp. I joined a non-denominational church where there was a mixture of every race. At this church, every single part of the service was timed. Twenty minutes for praise and worship and forty-five minutes for the Word of God and that was it. I think I stayed in that church until I was in my mid 30's. I started visiting a bible study at a C.O.G.I.C. church. I was then extended the invitation to come on Sunday for the worship service. I finally went. I looked up during prayer and several people were crying. When they read the scripture, people were crying. When the choir got up, they were crying even more. Even when the word of God was going forth, they were crying. The fact that everyone was crying made me comfortable enough to cry too. They began to tell me God loves me. Those words made me cry. This was the time where I began my long journey of church relationships and leadership positions. I never knew what a title could do to people. I began to love just being in the house of God. I grew so much spiritually. I became so close to so many women. I was Vice President of the Women's Department. I became the Women's Department President and Secretary as well as adjutant to our First Lady. Over 15 years of ministry, I loved it so much. Women can kill other women with our words, jealousy, and our issues. It has been said women cannot get along with each other. You can add me to the count because I believed this to be true. Serving in church with the spiritual gift of help can cause people to change. I walked away from the very thing I was gifted to do. Due to how I saw myself, the love, friendship, and ministry were all compromised because I felt I did not have what it took to be good enough to stand firm in my position. God had to change some things for me. All that I went through had to happen so that I could get to the point where I saw me. I had to start working on myself. I realized that situation had to happen to save my life. The feeling of failed friendships and connections felt as if it meant nothing when I walked away. It made me feel like I meant nothing to the people I called my friends.

Self-destruction was at an all-time high. I had been clinically diagnosed with depression. I was instructed by my doctor to go see a psychiatrist because of how severe the depression had become. Eventually I was prescribed different medications and put-on suicide watch. I was in a desperate place. I needed something different to help save my life. I began researching online topics like "how to save your life, how to live and not die and how to deal with past trauma." I found a Facebook Group called "I Survived on Purpose." I joined the Facebook group. The group was having a challenge, so I joined that too. The challenge had me so impressed that I stayed committed and I completed it. For the first time in my life, I invested in the growth of my own healing journey by investing in a life coach and healing classes.

At 52 years old I finally decided to fight for me. Finally, I put myself first. Working on myself was not easy at all. In fact, the hardest thing for me to do was to write a letter to myself. I had to tell myself that I loved me every day. I thought the coach's assignment was strange. Who writes letters to themselves? I did. In that letter, I found myself talking about friendships, my parents, my sisters, and everyone else except me. My coach had me write my letter over and talk to me. What a conversation that was. I never gave myself permission to do anything. I never told Stephanie "you are ok. I forgive you; you can make it." I never told myself to speak up and to not be scared. I never said, "you're beautiful!" How could I ever really have an amazing friendship without fear if I never spoke caring words to myself? I started to see the people that were in my life differently. I went from a person that felt as if I did not have any friends, to a person that knows I really do have people that love me for me. I started letting my heart heal and let God do His perfect work in my life. I learned something so profound "The end of something is the beginning of something else." I do not have to fear the ending of anything anymore because I anticipate what is next to come in my life. I started loving me. I started to get my hair done. I even got my lashes done. I felt cute. I said, "Girl you are beautiful!" I am finally in a space where I can let my voice be heard and speak with no fear. If you do not learn how to love yourself first and stop seeing yourself through your eyes you will never ever be able to see yourself through God's eyes. Hindsight is 20/20, as a child I thought my family was against me. Now that I am an adult, I realize that they were only doing what they knew to do at the time. I had to realize that my family could only love me based on the capacity that they were loved. I forgive them for the past. Most importantly I forgive myself. I am able to leave the past in the past and move on.

Now the BIG CHANGE!! I have the true sisterhood and friendships that were designed to be a healthy part of my life. Even family members are a major part of my life all because of how I see me. You do remember I said that I would never have anything to do with women, right? I have been blessed first to see that I have so much to offer women in my truth. In my time of solitude and quiet times I never knew God was recreating my entire life. So many disconnects had occurred because I just walked away and closed the door. God has reopened those doors on a completely new level and now it seems like I talk to women all day. I have been given an opportunity to return to some of those friends. Those real close friends that may not have returned if I continued in the old way. They now see the new me with a smile on my face and a clear mind. I love the women in my life!!! We break bread together, laugh, cry, raise our kids together and take trips. It feels good. This is true for the other women in this book. My God has smiled on me. They have learned more about me in one year than some people that have known me for 30 years. I thank God for transparency.

Offer your sisterhood a true connection from your heart, a love that you can agree to disagree on and still laugh in the next breath. A place where truth, love and disappointment can happen because you are human. True sisterhood is also where you can have those hard conversations without condemnation. Sisterhood offers you a way out where others may not understand.

Remember the way God sees you is what matters the most and you are perfect to Him and everything that you have gone through was according to the will of God. Living your life with an attitude of gratefulness will help you stay focused. Remember you are loved, and you are beautiful. You deserve all God has for you and sisterhood is one of the BEST parts.

Father God in the precious name of Jesus, I come boldly before your throne of grace. Thanking you and praising you for all that you do and all you continue to do. Dear God, I am asking that every person that reads this book finds the encouragement in their soul to understand that they are so deserving of true love and sisterhood. God you made us, and you know everything about us. Help us to understand and rely solely on you to give us the desires of our hearts. Father, those that are searching for love, searching for sisterhood and or have maybe even given up on true friendships has taken the time out to examine their hearts and have taken a deep closer look within themselves to make sure the pathway is clear to be authentically themself, and their hearts have been prepared to not only receive sisterhood but also do what it takes to give the same love in the same measure they expect to receive.

In Ephesians 3:20 NKJV says, Now to Him who is able to do exceedingly abundantly above all that we ask or think, according to the power that works in us. God, we look to you and we are confident we have the power within us to be true and authentic to ourselves first and to others that come across our paths. Just like you promised if we keep our minds stayed on you, you will keep us in perfect peace. Thank you, Father God, for every promise in our lives to be fulfilled. We thank you that love is who we are and as you continue to build us to be an example for the world to see we will take no glory for ourselves and we will say that you did it for us! You blessed us and we will be connected to sisterhood all over the world. Thank you for all that you have done and all that you continue to do. In Jesus Name,

Amen.

Stephanie Bell *is a leader and advocate globally for foster youth, caregivers and parents that are lost in state and county systems. Stephanie has a strong passion to help others rebuild and thrive in loving themselves. Stephanie is in the process of launching her life and travel coaching business to help others embrace self-care through the world of travel. Stephanie is excited to share her story of sisterhood based on her own life experiences with truth and transparency and is encouraged that she will help someone else believe in sisterhood. To contact Stephanie- Facebook.com/ stephanie.c.bell.1 | Instagram: @Praisehim2005*

Chapter 5

CLOSED MINDS DON'T GET FED
"The Secret of Being Open Minded"
By Polita Boyde

One's philosophy is not best expressed in words; it is expressed in the choices one makes. In the long run, we shape our lives, and we shape ourselves. The process never ends until we die. And the choices we make are ultimately our own responsibility. -Eleanor Roosevelt

When I was growing up I had very few female friendships. I was a tom-boy and I would hang young men quicker than I would the girls in my age group. I was also bullied and talked about so females were not my "thing." Through the years I have overcome that "I don't do females syndrome" that has been rooted in many women for centuries. Not only have I realized my own strength, but I am continuously encouraging women to find their inner strength and when we come together and get on one page, we can strike a mighty blow (one of my favorite lines from the movie Soul Food). By having an open mind, my entire perspective about women has shifted, and I have so many real sisters now because of it. I would not trade any of them for the world. This chapter is designed to do that for you. By the time you finish this chapter, I want you to have a completely different perception of the female species. I want you to be open-minded and consider being less guarded when it comes to networking and connecting with other women. I hope you have a true understanding of what sisterhood really means. Here is some food for thought, if you consider yourself to be a down to earth, loyal, trustworthy, encouraging, supportive and honest individual, and you heard someone say "I don't do females" or "women are messy" wouldn't you feel like they could be missing out on something great by not getting to know you?

For years, this one statement has dictated the way women view relationships with other women... "I don't do females." What does that even mean? The younger me would tell you it means that you purposely put yourself in a position to avoid friendships with women. It means that you have a guard up or have an apprehension about getting close to women. As I have gotten older, I realize that is probably one of the most childish, immature, and ignorant things I have ever heard. As I branch out into new experiences, I have discovered that one of the first things we must do before we follow through with our choices is to change our perception. Perception is the way we see things. Truth be told the perceptions we have had over the years about pursuing female friendships have more than likely been planted by someone else. Unfortunately, when this happens, we end up trying to figure out who we really are years later, and we end up reinventing ourselves. Well, guess what your perception has changed from what it was previously. Funny thing is the perception and thoughts that were also planted about female friendships are not even our own. Let us go back to the beginning for a minute, because I want to make sure you understand where this unnecessary discord between women came from. When sin entered the world in the garden, a plethora of thoughts, ideas, feelings, emotions, and desires entered in also. One of which was hatred.

> *Now Sarai Abram's wife bare him no children: and she had a handmaid, an Egyptian, whose name was Hagar. And Sarai said unto Abram, behold now, the Lord hath restrained me from bearing: I pray thee, go in unto my maid; it may be that I may obtain children by her. And Abram hearkened to the voice of Sarai.*
>
> *And Sarai Abram's wife took Hagar her maid the Egyptian, after Abram had dwelt ten years in the land of Canaan and gave her to her husband Abram to be his wife. And he went in unto Hagar, and she conceived: and when she saw that she had conceived, her mistress was despised in her eyes.*
> *(Genesis 16: 1-4)*

There are a couple of things I would like to point out in this passage.

First, I want to note Sarai's level of influence and power. As a woman you are designed to get results and that sometimes means doing the unthinkable and connecting with individuals you would not normally connect with. Everything you do is inspired by a thought, which eventually becomes a decision. You have the power to decide who you want to connect to. However, be open minded and mature enough to realize that the same connections you sometimes try to avoid are the very connections God designed to help push you to another level. Have you ever heard the expression, "closed mouths don't get fed?" It is basically a smart way of saying if an individual does not open their mouth and express what they want or need, the result is they get nothing. Bottom line is you cannot EXPECT to receive anything if you NEVER open your mouth, or your mind for that matter.

This same principle can work when it comes to the way you think about certain things. If you are closed minded and do not allow the possibility of anything new to be planted, grow and blossom then you are stunting your own growth and settling. How can you expect to grow into your full potential if you are not willing to open yourself up and allow others to get close to you? They may hold the key to your next level. I believe God secretly used this situation with Hagar to silently increase Sarai's faith. What happens if you decide you do not want to pursue a connection? In this case we are referring to female friendships or sisterhoods (notice I did not say associate or acquaintance). You may miss out on something significant, or you may end up going through a situation and that person was the glue that would have held you together, but "you don't do females."

The second thing I want to point out is how immediately after Hagar realized she was able to conceive she began looking at Sarai funny and giving her the side eye. Which brings me to my point about how discord was created between women in the first place. Once Hagar conceived, her thought process shifted to being better than Sarai because she was able to give Abram something his wife could not. These thoughts and emotions were released in the garden when Eve was deceived by the serpent. Once sin entered the world, the spirits of hatred, envy and jealousy also rose to the occasion. I am more than certain that Hagar is not the only woman who has ever given a side eye to someone just because they felt like they had a one up on another woman. The result here could have been completely different if Hagar and Sarai would have worked together in bringing up Ishmael. Although Isaac was the promise, he and his brother could have had some type of relationship. Sarai and Hagar could have been there to back one another up if they needed a mental break or just some me time. They could have developed a lifelong sisterhood and made sure that both of those boys always had a mother. I am just giving a few scenarios of what could have been although things happened the way they were probably intended to.

If I can be transparent, it took me a little while to be open when it came to building new friendships. I used to have the "no new friends" attitude also. What made the difference for me was I sought the Lord about what my next moves were and who I needed to be connected to in the process and it made things a lot easier. I remember in 2011 during a visit to this church in Old Hickory, TN, I was introduced to a young lady named Kayla and she had just become a mother to a beautiful baby girl. That was about all I remembered beside the fact that we resembled and could have been related. In 2012, I moved to Gallatin, TN with my ex-husband. Of course, with a new move comes anxiety, changes, nervousness, and growth. One of the areas I grew in quickly was meeting new people. I had somehow developed an extremely outgoing personality and literally did not meet a stranger. I guess you can say I adjusted to that "southern hospitality" effortlessly. One of the major transitions with moving was I started attending that same church I had visited in 2011 on a regular basis. I ended up becoming a member after a little while. After service on Sundays and Wednesdays I would mingle with some of the members and then make my way home. Then one random day after a Sunday or Wednesday service, Kayla and I connected and exchanged phone numbers. We started developing a relationship and became close. One day I was hanging with Kayla at her apartment and her younger cousin Jasmine came by and from that day forward we were always inseparable. About a year later, during one of our girls' days out I met another cousin Amber (they have a BIG family), and truth be told everything just fell together. I know it had to be a move of God because over the years I had prayed for God to remove anyone in my life that should not be there. Here we are 9 years later still going strong, keeping in touch, praying together, most importantly still sisters. I moved back to Indiana in 2018 and as bittersweet as it was, we never lost touch. In fact, in a sense we are closer now that we are all spread out. We make a point to have FaceTime girls' nights and we do Bible plan devotionals often. We have a text thread that we communicate in just about daily and we are always encouraging one another. The best part is that we can have individual relationships with one another and there is no friction, jealousy, or drama. I can honestly say connecting with these amazing women of God was my first real sisterhood experience and I would not trade them for anything.

I prayed that same prayer in the summer of 2019 and little did I know that my life was getting ready to unfold in a major way. That August, I joined this Facebook group AWAKEN! (look it up and join when you have a moment). I would scroll and read some of the content that was posted in the group, but one of the main things that caught my attention was the level of leadership and participation from the facilitators. They were always so open and literally right on my block when they did a live video or posted something in the group. On December 31, 2019, I was praying and writing things down in my journal about what I wanted to leave in 2019 and what I wanted to see in 2020. Most of the things I wrote were about moving to the next level that God had for me and really walking in my purpose. Little did I know that on January 9, 2020 my life was going to SHIFT. I received an inbox message from the lead facilitator of the group saying she wanted to speak with me. I was what I like to call "confuzzled" confused and puzzled. With no hesitation I set up the call and then boom, just like that my life went from operating in my own agenda to working for the kingdom of God in the realm of women empowerment.

Nakia Austin, lead facilitator of AWAKEN! an amazing woman of God changed my life that day. Did I mention we did not know one another? When she messaged me, she said my name came up in a meeting she had earlier that evening. She spoke to me about this ambassador program she was developing for the AWAKEN! group and this event that was in the works and she felt like I would be a good fit. Did I mention when I received the message, I had just come out of the prayer closet? I was immediately all in because I felt like God was showing me what my next level was. In March of 2020, I was reading "When Power Meets Potential" by TD Jakes and the confirmation I received was so unreal to me. As I read about the collision between Elijah and Elisha and that when Elijah threw his mantle on Elisha he ran after the purpose God had for him. The book described it as, are you ready…a spiritual AWAKENING. Now I am a bit extreme, but in that moment, I could see clearly exactly what was taking place. I was Elisha and Nakia was Elijah and this woman had thrown her mantle on me and it was up to me to decide if I wanted to chase after what God had for me.

While reading this book, God shed light on so many things. One of the revelations that stood out to me the most was how a stranger can hold the destiny that God has for me. I had known of Nakia and I would see her on FB live in the group, but I did not realize that being connected to her was unleashing a power that was deep on the inside of me. The second revelation was I had to decide to face the unknown, grow and move forward into what I felt was a move of God or if I wanted to stay comfortable and stagnant. There was a portion of the book that discussed how the Lord approached a couple of his disciples to move into their next, but they made excuses. They were verbally ready, but their hearts were still tied to things in their past. As you can see from this chapter, I made up my mind I was ready and made the leap to join the group of ambassadors. Hands down one of the best decisions I had ever made.

Here we sit almost a year later, and we have grown into an amazing sisterhood. The whole reason we decided to write this book was because our fearless leader's vision continues to manifest. Through her vision I have fallen in love with a passion I had all along… women empowerment and connection. The whole idea of women not being able to be friends and get along is so juvenile. It was not until I opened myself up to learning new things and people that I was able to launch my blog and my second business. I am building up my sisters and helping them become better versions of themselves. I find myself making a goal to compliment at least three women daily. I am constantly thinking about how I can advance the kingdom of God by displaying the love He displays to us daily. There is no judgement and no apprehension. God loves us just the way we are through all our faults and flaws. Can you imagine loving someone you have never met? I did not imagine it was possible, until I experienced it. The love, appreciation, and protection I had for these women I had only met through zoom and fb messenger had grown over one whole year. I found myself sharing things with them that my family does not even know because they get me. I found myself covering them in prayer and interceding on their behalf. It felt like walking into a Planet Fitness minus the working out, equipment and hydromassage. There is absolutely NO judgement. We encourage one another, pray together, joke around, cry together, and make plans just like we have known each other our whole lives.

Better is little with the fear of the Lord than a great treasure and trouble therewith. Proverbs 15:16

My secret to sisterhood is to be open minded. This scripture is the best way I can describe our sisterhood. Fearing the Lord and walking right into the next season of my life with six new sisters was a game changer for me. I sat one day thinking about how strategic God is and how he literally placed us together so that we can be a united front and a voice for women who have a fear of connecting with other women. Let me be honest, we had eleven ambassadors at one point and things did not work out for a few of them due to other circumstances. The authenticity we have in this group will not allow me to not share those details. The process of getting to know and share your vulnerabilities with new people is not easy, but it is for sure worth it. **Relationships of any capacity are going to be work. You must put in effort and look at what you can pour into it instead of what you can get out of it**. That is where I believe the blessing came from with our group. We all went in heart first and as servants and from that we have reaped the beauty of true friendship and sisterhood. I am grateful for my sisters, because at the end of the day if no one has my back I know for a fact I have six different women spread across the world that do. It truly means a lot to know you have people in your corner, cheering for you and wanting you to win. To know that God loves me so much that He not only blessed me to be part of something great, He gave me the gift and passion to share it with you in hopes that you stop procrastinating and connect with the right people. Do not allow pride and fear to derail your purpose. Get connected with your Elijah so you can move into your destiny. Be open minded in the process.

Prayer for an open mind
Heavenly Father, thank you for the person reading this. Thank you in advance for the desire they have to connect with women from different backgrounds and walks of life. Lord, I am asking that in this moment you would give my sister a new perspective and a new love for women. Not just the women she knows but those that you are going to add to her life. I pray that she will see that your desire for us as women was to never be petty, jealous, or hateful, but that we are to live together in unity. Your word says in Proverbs 17:17 that a friend is always loyal, and a brother is born in a time of need. Open my sister's mind to help her see that there are women who need her gift and talents. There are women in need of the anointing you have placed on my sister's life. You have directly and purposefully assigned people to her voice. I pray that she recognizes when you are moving her into new territories and new networks of women. I pray that you answer that silent cry all women have for a forever sisterhood. Lord, heal her heart from broken relationships so that she can be a vessel used for your honor and glory. I am asking on her behalf that you show her how to give and receive love the way you do. Grow her up and mature her in areas that may prevent her from developing long lasting sisterhoods with those you will send to pour into her life and minister to her. Lord, give her the confidence and courage to compliment and celebrate other women on their successes as she walks boldly and confidently in her own accomplishments. I pray that you continue to get the glory out of her life and that she will bless you for the remainder of her days. In Jesus Name
Amen.

Polita Boyde *(Lita B) is a creative entrepreneur, owner of Selegance LLC, and Lita B. Empowerment Educator, LLC. She started her entrepreneurial journey in 2018. Her vision is to be a beacon of light and servant to her clients. She also wants to be well-known in the event planning and life coaching industries. With her accomplishments including completion of her International Event and Wedding Planning Certification, Event Planning and Design Accreditation, and Master Life Coach certification, she plans to be a continued support system for her clientele serving the Southern and Midwest regions of Indiana. Having a passion for leadership, women empowerment, growth and development, and mentorship she has spent time cultivating troubled young women and the youth of the upcoming generations. Prior to her discovery of her love for event planning and passion for life coaching, she worked in the healthcare industry for 13 years holding various positions and has Bachelor of Science in Healthcare Administration. Polita has always been a passionate, driven and goal-oriented individual with a very nurturing spirit. She and her husband Keion were married in September 2019 and they have one son.*

To contact Polita - Email pboyde.923@gmail.com | On Facebook as Polita Boyde

Chapter 6

Girl, Put Yourself Out There...
Stop Denying the World of How Fabulous You Are!!
By Sonjia Lindsey

"But you are a chosen generation, a royal priesthood, a holy nation, His own special people, that you may proclaim the praises of Him who called you out of darkness into His marvelous light (1Peter 2:9)

You are special, you are unique…there is NO ONE like you. NO ONE who has your exact DNA. You have so much to offer the world. What is holding you back?

Past pain? Past hurt? Past is past …is it fear? False Evidence Appearing Real? Scripture tells us in 2 Timothy 1:7 (NKJV)

"For God has not given us a spirit of fear, but of power and of love and of a sound mind."

What is holding you back? What is making you feel that you are not worthy? Scripture tells us in Philippians 1:27 (NKJV)

"Only let your conduct be worthy of the gospel of Christ, so that whether I come and see you or am absent, I may hear of your affairs, that you stand fast in one spirit, with one mind striving together for the faith of the gospel,"

What was holding me back was my worth, or lack thereof. I was lacking in self-worth. I did not value myself. I believed that my validation came from others. I was looking at man, not God. I did not see myself as God saw me.

As I was growing up, I believed that I was not loved. My relationship with my mother was not the greatest. She was the one person who I thought should love me unconditionally. Instead, I was treated differently compared to my siblings. This led to low self-esteem, low self-worth and people pleasing. This was the beginning of me comparing myself to others. I wanted people to like me, to love me. I was afraid to speak up for myself, as I did not want to anger anyone. I allowed this to shape my life.

Why wasn't I good enough for love? Why wasn't I enough? What was wrong with me? I determined that I just was not worthy. I put myself on the bottom shelf, the clearance rack, if you will. I applied this mentality to all my "ships" whether it was relationships with males or friendships with females, coworkers, it did not matter to me, I thought that they were all better than me.

I believed I had friends. I convinced myself that they were as loyal to me as I was to them. I valued them. I was fearful that they would no longer be my friend if I did not agree with them and allow them to treat me like crap. I would like to share with you about two females I thought were my friends, "Leah" and "Mara".

I moved to a new town when I was 12. I went to a school that was clear across town from where I lived. I made a friend. Her name was "Leah". I would walk across town to Leah's house to play with her. She never came to my house. I always went to her. I told myself that there were more kids in her neighborhood than there were in mine and literally there was nothing to do. I also told myself that my mother would not have allowed her in the house anyway. We never had kids that came to "hang out" at our house. Over the years, this did not change. I still went to her. I was the one who would call. I was the one who would make the plans to go shopping, or out to eat. If it was something she wanted to do, I was all for it, just to make her happy. I trusted her. I shared secrets with her. She was not as forth coming. She wanted to know what was going on with me, without telling me what was going on with her. She got married, and let it slip that she was going to ask another friend to be in her wedding, not me. I was devastated because if it were me, I would not have done this to her. It was then that I started to realize that our "ship" was not as I once thought it was. I had been delusional and saw her as the person I wanted her to be, which was my friend.

I ignored the red flags. I would have people tell me she was not my friend. I did not want to hear it, but when you have someone coming back and telling you things you did not tell them, what else can you do but believe? She was the only person I told anything to. My trust was completely broken, and I was so hurt and angry. I started to back away. I was done. Then there was "Mara". We met when we were in junior high school. We were both interested in sports. When track season came around, she would pick me up on her bike, and give me rides to practice. We would sit together on the bus. After graduation, she moved away and got married. I would stay weekends at her house, and our kids would play together. We would attend church while we were at her house. She would also come to stay weekends at my house and bring her kids.

We kept in touch on and off over the years. When her daughter graduated, my kids and I went to celebrate her special day. As time went on, we did not visit as much but kept in touch. When my daughter graduated, I sent her an invitation for her party. I was looking forward to seeing her. By this time, she had gotten divorced, and started a new life for herself. The day of the party came and went. No word from her. My feelings were hurt. I did not understand why she would just ignore it. After a few days, I sent her a text, saying that my feelings were hurt that she did not come or even acknowledge the invitation. She responded that she was planning to surprise me with a visit, but since I sent her the text, she was not going to do it now and that I needed to pray.

I asked her what I had done. She did not reply. Instead, she blocked me on all social media, did not invite me to her wedding, and has not spoken to me since that day. Her family and I remain cool, as do her kids. Just not her. We do not mention her name. In Proverbs 17:17, it tells us,

"A friend loves at all times, and a brother is born for adversity."

My relationship with Leah and Mara were not healthy. They also were not bringing me closer to God. A friend that God has put in your life will bring you closer to Him. These friendships will thrive. There's respect and honesty. They will pray for you and with you.

I desperately wanted and believed I needed the validation of others. My friendships with females were one sided. I valued my friends, and I was not even a second thought to them. I would call, text, and be there when they needed whatever. When it came to my needs, they were neglected. They would decide when they wanted to talk to me and when they wanted take time to hang out with me. They hung out with their other friends and I was not invited. I started to compare myself to the other people they hung out with. And tried to behave more like them. The bible tells us in 2 Corinthians 10:12 (NKJV)

"For we dare not class ourselves or compare ourselves with those who commend themselves. But they, measuring themselves by themselves, and comparing themselves among themselves, are not wise".

I allowed myself to become a chameleon, adjusting to my environment. I was this person I though others wanted me to be. I had no clue who I was. My identity was gone. I went through a deep depression and avoided women because I believed they were all like my mother. Hurt people hurt people.

My low self-esteem allowed this behavior. If I spoke something in confidence to my friends, it was repeated. Add that to me not being able to trust anyone. Once I would get up the courage to say that something hurt my feelings, they would turn on me, and the friendship was done. Leaving me feeling dejected and once again, asking what is wrong with me.

I chose to be a single parent. I was unable to commit to anyone. I did not believe that I was worthy of being loved. I would tell myself that I wanted love, and when it came, I did not believe it, and I did not trust that it was real. How could someone possibly love me when my own mother did not? I ran away from it.

I started attending church. I did not grow up in church. There was no prayer in my house. We did not go to church as a family…except at Easter. My knowledge of God came from my paternal grandmother.

It was there that I met Ms. Ramsey. She had a heart for the Lord. I trusted her. Over time I became remarkably close to her. I trusted her so much that I became vulnerable enough to let the huge wall I had built around myself and my kids come down. I shared with her how I was raised, how my mother treated me. She became my surrogate mother and a grandmother to my two children. I became pregnant with my third, and it was time for me to go to the hospital. I needed to have a C-section. I was very overdue. I asked my mom to watch my kids while I was in the hospital. She told me no. I was in shock. She was the only one who lived in the same town as me, and I did not know where or who to turn to. I went to Ms. Ramsey. She said she would watch my babies. This was huge. She did not have kids in her home at the time. Her kids were all adults. I had comfort in knowing my kids were going to be taken care of. I had to admit to myself that I would not have been comfortable with my children staying with the woman who gave birth to me. Even though they were 12 and 6 at the time, that would have been a first for them. They had never been alone with her, not even for an hour. Even though she is their grandmother, they did not know her, they had not spent any time with her, so forget staying overnight.

Ms. Ramsey took my kids to school, made sure homework was completed at night, all the things that a mother would do. I had complications, and instead of being in the hospital for a couple of days, I ended up there for six. She did not complain. She just continued to love on my kids and be a blessing to us. The day I was released she came and cleaned my house for me and kept my kids for one more night so I could adjust to having a newborn in my home. She later shared with me that my kids included her in our nighttime ritual of saying "night, I love you." She declined payment for keeping my kids. When my kids needed a grandparent for school, she attended. She was such a huge blessing for my kids and me. Her love was unconditional. Through her, I learned that "biological" did not mean love and acceptance, but you could still have the love and acceptance through who God brings into your life.

It was important for me to know and recognize that when I was in need to allow someone in who was coming from a good place to love and encourage me. Through her, I was able to overcome that feeling of rejection from my mother. God brought into my life a mother. He gave my kids a grandmother who loved them unconditionally. Turning what could have been a generational curse into a generational blessing. Through the process of the pain and rejection, came a healing and acceptance of myself. Once I was able to love myself and believe I was worthy, I was able to walk confidently in the knowledge that God loved me. This was a turning point for me. My focus went from pleasing everyone around me, to only pleasing God. In everything I did, for His glory. The friendships that I once craved, I was no longer interested in. Instead, God brought women into my life who were about serving Him.

John 15:11-15 NKJV

"These things I have spoken to you, that My joy may remain in you, and that your joy may be full. [12] This is My commandment, that you love one another as I have loved you. [13] Greater love has no one than this, than to lay down one's life for his friends. [14] You are My friends if you do whatever I command you. [15] No longer do I call you servants, for a servant does not know what his master is doing; but I have called you friends, for all things that I heard from My Father I have made known to you.

This allowed me to be able to open up to the sisterhood of 100 Healed. This allowed me to understand that hurt people hurt people. This allowed me to open up to women and look forward to having true, honest friendships. Accepting myself has helped me to accept others for who they are. Coming out of that dark place I was in for a period of my life, allowed me to be able to reach out to women with a pure heart.

Jeremiah 1:4-6
4 Then the word of the Lord came to me, saying:
5 "Before I formed you in the womb I knew you.
Before you were born I sanctified[a] you;
I [b]ordained you a prophet to the nations."

My Secret to Sisterhood: Allow God to bring the people He wants in your life, so you can thrive. You do not have to allow yourself to be disrespected to have friends.

My prayer for you dear Sister:
Dear Lord, teach me to love others the way you first loved me. As I build relationships let them see You in all that I do. Thank You for removing those out of my life that were not a part of where You are taking me. As You continue to bring the people into my life, those that honor You, I thank You Father for knowing who and what I need. All these things are only possible through You, the God who abides with me and calls me friend.

Amen.

Sonjia Lindsey *resides in Ohio and is passionate about helping others, giving, and leading by example. She has a heart for building and encouraging others. She holds degrees in Healthcare Administration and Cancer Management. Sonjia is also a Court Appointed Special Advocate, the voice for children. In her free time she loves creating memories with her family, reading, and going to the beach with her dog. Sonjia is very active in her church, Cedar Creek, and enjoys growing in her faith.*
To contact Sonjia - Email: srlindsey01@hotmail.com

Chapter 7

The Divine Gift of Godly Relationships
By Tempy Douglas

"Are you done yet?" I will never forget those words. My dear friend, who even now I still call "My Theresa" with tears in her eyes, asked me this question almost 17 years ago. Theresa came home from work to find me asleep on her sofa. "I never lock my front door" I remember her telling me this as I sat in detox for the third or fourth time, that cold February day. I was counting on that door being unlocked. I met Theresa at The Women's Healing Place, a rehab in Louisville. She was a counselor in detox, checking in women like me that struggled with alcohol and drug addiction.

I would sit beside her desk, not talking, just watching the women coming in and out of detox. I just wanted to be left alone. I was angry at these women and angry at myself for being called one of them! As I sat beside Theresa's desk, she would tell the women to hug each other and to hug me. I would cringe, stiffening my body at their touch; I refused to return their hugs. Theresa would smile or laugh gently like she had a secret. The more they hugged me, the angrier I became. I thought, " I wish they would leave me alone! What is Theresa smiling about?" I was not one of them; they were not my friends and definitely not my family! The only thing we had in common was that we could not stop getting high! BUT! The difference between them and I was that I was not an addict. I used it recreationally. I could stop when I wanted to. This time I smiled to myself, shaking my head.

Our backgrounds may have been different with few similarities. Some of us were mothers, daughters, grandmothers; some of us had jobs, I was teaching. Some were nurses, caregivers; several were detox counselors that relapsed! The biggest similarity, none of us wanted to die! I had heard stories of addicts and alcoholics overdosing after being robbed, their bodies thrown outside or in dumpsters. Our addiction was having its way, at least theirs was, not mine. "My Theresa" would look at me and tell these women, "Hug her! She needs you to love on her; we all do" I kept asking myself," what in the hell does she keep smiling for!"? I continued to pull back from their hugs, not knowing that one day these hugs would be my lifeline. Their hugs would be a divine respirator that would bring me back to life! A precious possession.

I would one day realize our love for each other would last a lifetime. Thank GOD, we are our sister's keeper! As I sat in detox and attended daily NA and AA meetings, I watched the eyes of these women slowly open with wonder; some were smiling, "Ok, all this smiling is getting on my nerves!" Could it be that they finally realized that their lives had a purpose, had meaning! Did their eyes remind them that GOD still cared? The loving, forgiving GOD had not forgotten about us! The more compassionate the presence of GOD, the less acute our pain? My eyes wanted to see what they were seeing. I wanted to feel what they were feeling. These women wanted to love me until I learned to love myself. They trusted me until I could trust myself. Time spent letting GOD'S love and their love flow through me would one day be an investment in eternity. I would one day learn, women are built for connection, and GOD entrusts us with the care of each other's heart. We are really our sister's keeper!

I did not trust them. I did not want to love them or want them to love me! Yes, I love GOD, but did He still love me? The women told me, "Tempy, the answers you seek would never come unless you change your mind and change your mindset." I knew my mind was in total chaos. I was on the hunt for who I could not find, ME! My heart and soul were in turmoil. Regardless of success or failure, pain or joy, a new life of endless possibilities was available, only if I could surrender. At least that is what they told me. I could not trust a word they said. I continued to be angry because I would have to fight hard to get what they had. I did not plan on staying in detox forever. Was I angry at the person I had become, or was I more afraid of the person GOD wanted me to be? "My Theresa" and these "sisters" continued to encourage me. I remember one of the" old timers" (a woman with a substantial amount of sobriety), telling me, "Tempy, you are suffering from a great deal of needless guilt and a lot of resentment. GOD lays out tougher paths for many of us, and you sis, are treading on one tough path. GOD has the power to interrupt your life and turn it upside down. But GOD would not have put you on this path if He did not think you could handle it! You must share this path of righteousness with those you love and with those who love you; it is called Kingdom Business!!"

She went on to say, "Tempy, GOD is not asking you to be perfect. Just be grateful that you have been chosen! It is ok to be hurting, angry, even afraid. Like many of us, you feel resentful toward others and yourself. Tempy, recovery is like labor pains. To give birth to your new life, you will feel the pains of addiction before the birth of recovery!"

She continued, "Let your 'sisters' hold your hand through this painful delivery. This is the emotional turmoil experienced before you give birth to the joy of peace and serenity. Let your 'sisters' share your joy. Through the pains, you will not be alone. Put your hand in our hands and together, we can make it!! Hold your head up to the light, GOD'S amazing light. Even if just for the moment you do not see, keep looking, but take one day at a time!"

I found myself thinking, could these" sisters" really identify with my pain and my struggles? Could we have a mutual kinship with each other, not competing, but completing each other? They knew I had dreams of a new life; they also had these dreams. Their relationship with me and other "newcomers" was designed to take us to the next level. If we gave them the chance, they would help make our dreams come true. These sisters were motivated by love. GOD'S unconditional love. GOD'S divine unconditional love. They were "chosen" by GOD to love me, despite me. We were GOD'S work of art, "fearfully and wonderfully made." These women that I called "sisters" assured us that GOD'S grace was as much with us as it was with them!

"Grace! Mercy!!" When I was getting high, crying, begging GOD to help me, where was GOD'S grace and mercy? I would beg GOD to have mercy and let me die, that would have been the GRACIOUS thing to do, but no, I'm still here, with you, my so-called 'sisters'... I continued to find fault with these women, still possessed by anger, hostility, and resentment. My self-will ran riot; my old pattern of behavior was screaming inside me, threatening to explode. But deep down inside, I found the "grace" to restrain myself. Secretly, in my mind, I told myself I could levitate above all of them, my will was all-powerful, my mind told me I was in control, I could reject their GOD-GIVEN nature, their love, their sisterhood! The negativity of my drug-induced mindset told me I could control every aspect of my life, my very soul. My mental self-destruction had set in motion this malady of misfortunes that I did not deserve. I dared not draw closer to these women who kept calling me their sister, but they were determined to draw closer to me, determined to love me back to life.

I could remember at the in-house meetings, standing in the circle, we would hold hands and pray, "let us pray for the suffering Addict in and out of this circle," was I one of the "suffering addicts" these sisters were praying for? I was still filled with resentment that led to my unhappiness. This resentment toward others was deeply rooted in the resentment of myself. "Resentment can destroy you; it's the primary cause of relapse. It not only causes mental and physical illness, but it will also make you physically ill", I continued to hear the voices of the sisters in my head! I was not really holding a grudge against them; I was beating others with the club of resentment that I needed to use on myself!

Why was I so afraid to connect with these women, these sisters? They were there to help me to release this unbearable anger, this need to resent others, this need to resent myself! "My Theresa" told me on one of my many trips to detox, "Tempy, you are not just living to be drug-free; you are living to love and to serve others. You cannot keep what you have unless you give it away! When are you going to use GOD'S grace to keep on living?" Was I losing my ability to choose life? I was a victim of compulsion that would eventually lead me to my own self-destruction. But my addiction was bigger than my willpower; I wasn't on the road to freedom. Was this the beginning of the end?

After 90 days in rehab, my disease won, telling me I was cured. I left the Women's Healing Place. I believed I had become free and would begin a perfect path of righteousness. But the sisters had warned me it did not work that way. "Tempy, you will make mistakes; you may humiliate yourself by succumbing to incomprehensible demoralizing behavior to get drugs. But one day, sis, you will realize these mistakes will be a necessary part of your journey." If I wanted to live, I had to be free of anger, fear, and pride-filled resentment. There was a new life of endless possibilities, if I surrendered and with their love and prayers, I would never be alone again GOD had blessed my life with Divine GODLY Connections, GODLY Relationships with a family, the sisters I had left behind.

The gift of sisterhood is a treasure not to be taken lightly. We are like angels to one another; we must lift our sister up when her wings have trouble remembering how to fly; put your hand in my hand and together we can make it. Only by being willing to take advice and accept direction could I set foot on the road to straight thinking, solid honesty, and genuine humility. Only then could I enjoy these gifts of GODLINESS.

I had to trust the infinite GOD rather than my finite self! For GOD to use me I had to change my mindset, leave my comfort zone, I was so afraid, I did not know what to expect. But in order for GOD to use me, I had to be afraid! Suffering can have a divine purpose, GOD loves us so much, He can get in our way! I could not be afraid of pain. Sometimes you must have pain before you have peace!

For seven years of self-inflicted pain, I had shut myself off from the sunlight of the spirit. What could I do to come out of this darkness, my self-inflicted blindness? Intellectually I could accept that I had a problem; emotionally, I could not. How could I admit that I wanted, that I needed these sisters in my life? My resentfulness told me humility was another name for weakness. But I had a moment of clarity that reminded me that humility and intellect are compatible, provided I put humility first! At the forefront of my mind, I knew addiction was no recreational fun and games. I knew I had a problem. I could not stop using drugs. I knew I needed help. I knew I could not do it alone. I had to accept my circumstances as they were. What could I do? What would I do if I were not afraid? I was powerless. I was suffering alone. I was sitting in a house with a room full of people I did not really know. I just watched them. Occasionally, someone would say something to me, but I did not hear them; I was in a house. I did not know who it belonged to. I was feeling confused and alone. I had the notion that I could still live a normal life. I felt that I could do this alone; maybe asking GOD to help me now and then, this notion, this INSANITY, slowly began to evaporate! I realized that in refusing to put GOD first I had deprived myself of His help.

GOD has a way of keeping us, blessing us, despite the hell we put ourselves through! Even when I cried out in anger against GOD, I was still calling on GOD, My GOD! Even through the anger, the resentment, the fear, GOD was still my GOD! He promised me "goodness and mercy would follow me all the days of my life." GOD keeps His promises. I prayed for GOD'S hand to take control. GOD did what He does best, He answered. GOD'S timing is perfect; He froze the lies that I told myself, so I could know the truth. The truth that I was an addict. The truth of recovery and redemption. So great is GOD'S faithfulness. GOD'S grace, His presence has kept me safe in the most difficult and dangerous situations in my life. I have remained silent because I was consumed by resentment, guilt, and fear. I was consumed by embarrassment. And despite my self-inflicted challenges, GOD remained faithful. The enemy wanted to keep me in a cycle of shame. The parts of my life that are so painful to me will be the very areas that GOD would use to set me free. I want GOD to get the glory for how I live now.

No one enters your life accidentally. I did not realize when I walked into "My Theresa's" house almost 17 years ago on 2/10/2004 that I walked into her life and her heart. I did not realize when I walked into the Women's Healing Place I was walking into a place that would heal me. Theresa's smile, her quiet, gentle laughter meant that she understood what I could not say even when my thoughts could not form the words. The continuous hugs and always "I love you sis" was the power to take away the pain that threatened to destroy me. These hurtful emotions that kept me in bondage for 7 years had a divine purpose. These emotions were the stepping stones to recovery, a road to freedom.

I realized then that I could not be healed without the help of women, Sisters like me. I had to try and forget everything I thought I knew and trust my sisters because I could not trust myself. I had to believe that I would never be alone again. Such is the paradox of sisterhood, the divine gift of godly relationships, is what I had. We had a relationship because of our trials and tests. Change is the essence of a new life, but we must be willing to admit complete defeat because if nothing changes, nothing changes! Our recovery must come first so that everyone and everything else in our lives will not come last. Our lives, our stories are a road map to healing others. GOD sustains us through every season of our lives. As sisters, we will impact the next generation. Our stories, mistakes, our challenges are areas of healing. Our stories provide encouragement and hope for our sisters going through similar struggles. GOD equips us with boldness to share our testimony with confidence and conviction. Our sisterhood will remind other sisters we are not alone. Knowing you are not alone provides comfort to your spirit. True sisterhood can help you dismantle the feeling of isolation. Their experience helped shape me into the GODLY woman I am today. Our sisterhood serves as a witness to who GOD is. We are a testament to GOD'S faithfulness. The best way to show gratefulness is to accept everything, even our problems with joy. Sisterhood can become the face of grace, delight, and mercy- the face of GOD in each other. Our love for each other builds a strong bridge. We can grow separately without ever growing apart.

On February 10, 2021, I celebrated 17 years of sobriety and 17 years of being drug-free. "My Theresa", my counselors from the Women's Healing Place are my sisters, my family. I have formed a loving relationship with my sisters in 100 Healed; I am called" Auntie" by many of them. I love this! I have lost loved ones on this journey, including my own baby sister, Barbara. Memories past and present of beloved family and friends will live in my heart forever. That is one of the beautiful things about sisterhood. You have family all over the world. Sisterhood beckoned me to the arms of other women, who have become my family. I could not become who I wanted to be by remaining who I was. I could not survive alone; GOD sent heavenly help, Sisters that inspired and encouraged me. The best healers are wounded healers, Sisters that can turn their trauma and drama into testimonies. GOD does not want to waste anything, not even our scars. Our scars are a reminder that we are survivors. I found my own strength and courage. GOD took my hand and placed it in the hands of my sisters. I can feel the love of GOD radiate from these strong women. I thank GOD for the Marys, Elizabeths, Naomis and Ruths; He put in my life!

When you need to change your mindset, heart, and soul, it is crucial to have the love and support of divine relationships. GOD does his best work by using other people, sisters who have shown me and can show you the way. The paradox of sisterhood is the encouragement from our sisters that can change the course of our life. She is the sister that joyfully sings with you when you are on the mountain top and silently walks beside you in the valley. She is the sister whose love focuses on your inner soul; she sees you need help and sets her compassion to work for you. She is the sister whose love is a divine connection from GOD that gives, knows, and lasts!

My sisters, there is beauty in our brokenness! Our stories provide hope for the hopeless and a home for healing. Our stories are significant and incredibly valuable to GOD'S kingdom. My sisters, it was good for me to be afflicted! I am grateful there is gratitude in my affliction. Life took me from the mountain top to the valley. I was hopeless and homeless. I was the least, the lost and the left out. I was in the valley and could not find my way out. BUT GOD...I did not know that the valley was a place of preparation where GOD wanted me to grow! I grew in that valley and I would not take anything for my journey!! The one thing that made me hold on was that I did not want to let GOD down! My dear sisters, a shift is coming our way. Do not be afraid to walk through your valley, "Yea thou you walk through the valley...fear no evil!" GOD is our constant, cosmic companion! GOD will heal us in the valley! You will be reminded that you are a survivor! We are built for this. Every moment in our lives prepared us for this moment! GOD sustains us through every season. GOD has put sisters in our life to help us guide and direct each other. I am the consequence of such love and support. When I accepted my circumstances as coming from GOD, I realized it was directly sent and permissively allowed! My sisters, we do not always get to choose when we suffer, but GOD will get the glory out of every tear we shed! May we never forget: We Need GOD on our best day as desperately as we need

GOD on our worst! Tell GOD your needs and do not forget to thank Him for His answers. If we are willing, GOD IS ABLE.

Most loving GOD, we ask your blessings and protection for all who suffer from the dis-ease of addiction. Strengthen each sister to reach out for help from You, LORD GOD, and from each other. Enable us to take the first step to admit we are powerless, and our life is unmanageable. Bless our sisterhood with the persistence to persevere. Help us with the determination to be set free, help us LORD GOD to turn our gloomy days to glorious days. You are the GOD of grace and mercy; we thank you that your mercy has no expiration date. We get tired LORD, but strengthen us with EXPLOSIVE POWER not to quit, because you've reminded us, our sisterhood, we are right around the corner from our breakthrough! Thank You GOD for meeting us where we are, but not leaving us where You found us! Our faith and trust in You are now the antidote for our fear and anxiety, LORD, you will not allow our destiny to be destroyed by our history, help us to use our past to prepare us for our future. LORD GOD, help us to restore the broken hearts and broken dreams of our sisters, help us LORD GOD to triumph over our tragedies, "bestow (on Our Sisterhood), a crown of beauty instead of ashes, the oil of gladness instead of mourning, a garment of praise instead of despair"(Isaiah 61:3) The word that You speak gives our sisterhood life! We realize LORD GOD, we may not be where we want to be, but we are IN THE PROCESS OF BECOMING!! We are willing, GOD IS ABLE.... Amen.

Tempy Douglas is a retired Special Needs Instructor, a Mother, Grandmother, Sister and Daughter. One of her biggest achievements thus far is becoming a grateful recovering addict. She is blessed to be a part of The Secrets to Sisterhood Anthology. Her story is one of pain and perseverance, fear, and faith. Her story is one of darkness and determination. In her darkest hour she listened, and GOD gave her a precious message from her sisters who were addicts like herself that lead her to the light. They helped her realize WE ARE ALL OUR SISTER'S KEEPER!
To contact Tempy - Email: tempydouglas@gmail.com

The 7 Secrets of Sisterhood

1. My secret to sisterhood is to always be willing to have the hard conversations. Don't think about the conversation too much in your head before you talk because it could cause you to back pedal. If your sisters are true friends, they will be open to listen to you. You will both be able to voice your concerns and come out with a new understanding of one another. There is nothing that a good conversation can't solve. -**Sharice Porter**

2. My secret to maintaining healthy relationships is to lead with empathy and be transparent with your emotions. - **Bridgette Smith**

3. One of the secrets of sisterhood is to embrace one another's differences, not to be jealous or envious of them. Celebrate each other's accomplishments. – **Charity Todd**

4. Offer your sisterhood a true connection from your heart, a love that you can agree to disagree on and still laugh in the next breath. A place where truth, love and disappointment can happen because you are human. True sisterhood is also where you can have those hard conversations without condemnation. Sisterhood offers you a way out where others may not understand. -**Stephanie Cherise Bell**

5. Relationships of any capacity are going to be work. You must put in effort and look at what you can pour into it instead of what you can get out of it. -**Polita Boyde**

6. Allow God to bring the people He wants in your life, so you're able to thrive. You do not have to allow yourself to be disrespected to have friends. -**Sonjia Lindsey**

7. The gift of sisterhood is a treasure not to be taken lightly. We are like angels to one another; we must lift our sister up when her wings have trouble remembering how to fly; put your hand in my hand and together we can make it. -**Tempy Douglas**

www.ingramcontent.com/pod-product-compliance
Lightning Source LLC
Chambersburg PA
CBHW071332190426
43193CB00041B/1750